Lady Windermere's Fan

A PLAY ABOUT A GOOD WOMAN

Oscar Wilde

HAWK PRESS

Published by

Hawk Press
4836/24, Ansari Road, Daryaganj
New Delhi – 110 002
Phones : 9643330713, +91-11-23278618, +91-11-35676207
E-mail: thehawkpress@gmail.com
www.thehawkpress.com

ISBN : 978-93-92322-65-5

TO

THE DEAR MEMORY

OF

ROBERT EARL OF LYTTON

IN AFFECTION

AND

ADMIRATION

THE PERSONS OF THE PLAY

Lord Windermere

Lord Darlington

Lord Augustus Lorton

Mr. Dumby

Mr. Cecil Graham

Mr. Hopper

Parker, Butler

Lady Windermere

The Duchess of Berwick

Lady Agatha Carlisle

Lady Plymdale

Lady Stutfield

Lady Jedburgh

Mrs. Cowper-Cowper

Mrs. Erlynne

Rosalie, Maid

FIRST ACT

SCENE

Morning-room of Lord Windermere's house in Carlton House Terrace. Doors C. and R. Bureau with books and papers R. Sofa with small tea-table L. Window opening on to terrace L. Table R.

[Lady Windermere is at table R., arranging roses in a blue bowl.]

[Enter Parker.]

Parker. Is your ladyship at home this afternoon?

Lady Windermere. Yes—who has called?

Parker. Lord Darlington, my lady.

Lady Windermere. [Hesitates for a moment.] Show him up—and I'm at home to any one who calls.

Parker. Yes, my lady.

[Exit C.]

Lady Windermere. It's best for me to see him before to-night. I'm glad he's come.

[Enter Parker C.]

Parker. Lord Darlington,

[Enter Lord Darlington C.]

[Exit Parker.]

Lord Darlington. How do you do, Lady Windermere?

Lady Windermere. How do you do, Lord Darlington? No, I can't shake hands with you. My hands are all wet with these roses. Aren't they lovely? They came up from Selby this morning.

Lord Darlington. They are quite perfect. [Sees a fan lying on the table.] And what a wonderful fan! May I look at it?

Lady Windermere. Do. Pretty, isn't it! It's got my name on it, and everything. I have only just seen it myself. It's my husband's birthday present to me. You know to-day is my birthday?

Lord Darlington. No? Is it really?

Lady Windermere. Yes, I'm of age to-day. Quite an important day in my life, isn't it? That is why I am giving this party to-night. Do sit down. [Still arranging flowers.]

Lord Darlington. [Sitting down.] I wish I had known it was your birthday, Lady Windermere. I would have covered the whole street in front of your house with flowers for you to walk on. They are made for you.

[A short pause.]

Lady Windermere. Lord Darlington, you annoyed me last night at the Foreign Office. I am afraid you are going to annoy me again.

Lord Darlington. I, Lady Windermere?

[Enter Parker and Footman C., with tray and tea things.]

Lady Windermere. Put it there, Parker. That will do. [Wipes her hands with her pocket-handkerchief, goes to tea-table, and sits down.] Won't you come over, Lord Darlington?

[Exit Parker C.]

Lord Darlington. [Takes chair and goes across L.C.] I am quite miserable, Lady Windermere. You must tell me what I did. [Sits down at table L.]

Lady Windermere. Well, you kept paying me elaborate compliments the whole evening.

Lord Darlington. [Smiling.] Ah, nowadays we are all of us so hard up, that the only pleasant things to pay are compliments. They're the only things we can pay.

Lady Windermere. [Shaking her head.] No, I am talking

very seriously. You mustn't laugh, I am quite serious. I don't like compliments, and I don't see why a man should think he is pleasing a woman enormously when he says to her a whole heap of things that he doesn't mean.

Lord Darlington. Ah, but I did mean them. [Takes tea which she offers him.]

Lady Windermere. [Gravely.] I hope not. I should be sorry to have to quarrel with you, Lord Darlington. I like you very much, you know that. But I shouldn't like you at all if I thought you were what most other men are. Believe me, you are better than most other men, and I sometimes think you pretend to be worse.

Lord Darlington. We all have our little vanities, Lady Windermere.

Lady Windermere. Why do you make that your special one? [Still seated at table L.]

Lord Darlington. [Still seated L.C.] Oh, nowadays so many conceited people go about Society pretending to be good, that I think it shows rather a sweet and modest disposition to pretend to be bad. Besides, there is this to be said. If you pretend to be good, the world takes you very seriously. If you pretend to be bad, it doesn't. Such is the astounding stupidity of optimism.

Lady Windermere. Don't you want the world to take you seriously then, Lord Darlington?

Lord Darlington. No, not the world. Who are the people the world takes seriously? All the dull people one can think of, from the Bishops down to the bores. I should like you to take me very seriously, Lady Windermere, you more than any one else in life.

Lady Windermere. Why—why me?

Lord Darlington. [After a slight hesitation.] Because I think we might be great friends. Let us be great friends. You may want a friend some day.

Lady Windermere. Why do you say that?

Lord Darlington. Oh!—we all want friends at times.

Lady Windermere. I think we're very good friends already, Lord Darlington. We can always remain so as long as you don't—

Lord Darlington. Don't what?

Lady Windermere. Don't spoil it by saying extravagant silly things to me. You think I am a Puritan, I suppose? Well, I have something of the Puritan in me. I was brought up like that. I am glad of it. My mother died when I was a mere child. I lived always with Lady Julia, my father's elder sister, you know. She was stern to me, but she taught me what the world is forgetting, the difference that there is between what is right and what is wrong. She allowed of no compromise. I allow of none.

Lord Darlington. My dear Lady Windermere!

Lady Windermere. [Leaning back on the sofa.] You look on me as being behind the age.—Well, I am! I should be sorry to be on the same level as an age like this.

Lord Darlington. You think the age very bad?

Lady Windermere. Yes. Nowadays people seem to look on life as a speculation. It is not a speculation. It is a sacrament. Its ideal is Love. Its purification is sacrifice.

Lord Darlington. [Smiling.] Oh, anything is better than being sacrificed!

Lady Windermere. [Leaning forward.] Don't say that.

Lord Darlington. I do say it. I feel it—I know it.

[Enter Parker C.]

Parker. The men want to know if they are to put the carpets on the terrace for to-night, my lady?

Lady Windermere. You don't think it will rain, Lord Darlington, do you?

Lord Darlington. I won't hear of its raining on your birthday!

Lady Windermere. Tell them to do it at once, Parker.

[Exit Parker C.]

Lord Darlington. [Still seated.] Do you think then—of course I am only putting an imaginary instance—do you think that in the case of a young married couple, say about two years married, if the husband suddenly becomes the intimate friend of a woman of—well, more than doubtful character—is always calling upon her, lunching with her, and probably paying her bills—do you think that the wife should not console herself?

Lady Windermere. [Frowning.] Console herself?

Lord Darlington. Yes, I think she should—I think she has the right.

Lady Windermere. Because the husband is vile—should the wife be vile also?

Lord Darlington. Vileness is a terrible word, Lady Windermere.

Lady Windermere. It is a terrible thing, Lord Darlington.

Lord Darlington. Do you know I am afraid that good people do a great deal of harm in this world. Certainly the greatest harm they do is that they make badness of such extraordinary importance. It is absurd to divide people into good and bad. People are either charming or tedious. I take the side of the charming, and you, Lady Windermere, can't help belonging to them.

Lady Windermere. Now, Lord Darlington. [Rising and crossing R., front of him.] Don't stir, I am merely going to finish my flowers. [Goes to table R.C.]

Lord Darlington. [Rising and moving chair.] And I must say I think you are very hard on modern life, Lady Windermere. Of course there is much against it, I admit. Most women, for instance, nowadays, are rather mercenary.

Lady Windermere. Don't talk about such people.

Lord Darlington. Well then, setting aside mercenary people,

who, of course, are dreadful, do you think seriously that women who have committed what the world calls a fault should never be forgiven?

Lady Windermere. [Standing at table.] I think they should never be forgiven.

Lord Darlington. And men? Do you think that there should be the same laws for men as there are for women?

Lady Windermere. Certainly!

Lord Darlington. I think life too complex a thing to be settled by these hard and fast rules.

Lady Windermere. If we had 'these hard and fast rules,' we should find life much more simple.

Lord Darlington. You allow of no exceptions?

Lady Windermere. None!

Lord Darlington. Ah, what a fascinating Puritan you are, Lady Windermere!

Lady Windermere. The adjective was unnecessary, Lord Darlington.

Lord Darlington. I couldn't help it. I can resist everything except temptation.

Lady Windermere. You have the modern affectation of weakness.

Lord Darlington. [Looking at her.] It's only an affectation, Lady Windermere.

[Enter Parker C.]

Parker. The Duchess of Berwick and Lady Agatha Carlisle.

[Enter the Duchess of Berwick and Lady Agatha Carlisle C.]

[Exit Parker C.]

Duchess of Berwick. [Coming down C., and shaking hands.] Dear Margaret, I am so pleased to see you. You remember Agatha, don't you? [Crossing L.C.] How do you do, Lord Darlington? I won't let you know my daughter, you are far too wicked.

Lord Darlington. Don't say that, Duchess. As a wicked man I am a complete failure. Why, there are lots of people who say I have never really done anything wrong in the whole course of my life. Of course they only say it behind my back.

Duchess of Berwick. Isn't he dreadful? Agatha, this is Lord Darlington. Mind you don't believe a word he says. [Lord Darlington crosses R.C.] No, no tea, thank you, dear. [Crosses and sits on sofa.] We have just had tea at Lady Markby's. Such bad tea, too. It was quite undrinkable. I wasn't at all surprised. Her own son-in-law supplies it. Agatha is looking forward so much to your ball to-night, dear Margaret.

Lady Windermere. [Seated L.C.] Oh, you mustn't think it is going to be a ball, Duchess. It is only a dance in honour of my birthday. A small and early.

Lord Darlington. [Standing L.C.] Very small, very early, and very select, Duchess.

Duchess of Berwick. [On sofa L.] Of course it's going to be select. But we know that, dear Margaret, about your house. It is really one of the few houses in London where I can take Agatha, and where I feel perfectly secure about dear Berwick. I don't know what society is coming to. The most dreadful people seem to go everywhere. They certainly come to my parties—the men get quite furious if one doesn't ask them. Really, some one should make a stand against it.

Lady Windermere. I will, Duchess. I will have no one in my house about whom there is any scandal.

Lord Darlington. [R.C.] Oh, don't say that, Lady Windermere. I should never be admitted! [Sitting.]

Duchess of Berwick. Oh, men don't matter. With women it is different. We're good. Some of us are, at least. But we are positively getting elbowed into the corner. Our husbands would really forget our existence if we didn't nag at them from time to time, just to remind them that we have a perfect legal right to do so.

Lord Darlington. It's a curious thing, Duchess, about the game of marriage—a game, by the way, that is going out of fashion—the wives hold all the honours, and invariably lose the odd trick.

Duchess of Berwick. The odd trick? Is that the husband, Lord Darlington?

Lord Darlington. It would be rather a good name for the modern husband.

Duchess of Berwick. Dear Lord Darlington, how thoroughly depraved you are!

Lady Windermere. Lord Darlington is trivial.

Lord Darlington. Ah, don't say that, Lady Windermere.

Lady Windermere. Why do you talk so trivially about life, then?

Lord Darlington. Because I think that life is far too important a thing ever to talk seriously about it. [Moves up C.]

Duchess of Berwick. What does he mean? Do, as a concession to my poor wits, Lord Darlington, just explain to me what you really mean.

Lord Darlington. [Coming down back of table.] I think I had better not, Duchess. Nowadays to be intelligible is to be found out. Good-bye! [Shakes hands with Duchess.] And now—[goes up stage] Lady Windermere, good-bye. I may come to-night, mayn't I? Do let me come.

Lady Windermere. [Standing up stage with Lord Darlington.] Yes, certainly. But you are not to say foolish, insincere things to people.

Lord Darlington. [Smiling.] Ah! you are beginning to reform me. It is a dangerous thing to reform any one, Lady Windermere. [Bows, and exit C.]

Duchess of Berwick. [Who has risen, goes C.] What a charming, wicked creature! I like him so much. I'm quite delighted he's gone! How sweet you're looking! Where do you get your gowns? And now I must tell you how sorry I am for you, dear Margaret. [Crosses to sofa and sits with Lady Windermere.] Agatha, darling!

Lady Agatha. Yes, mamma. [Rises.]

Duchess of Berwick. Will you go and look over the photograph album that I see there?

Lady Agatha. Yes, mamma. [Goes to table up L.]

Duchess of Berwick. Dear girl! She is so fond of photographs of Switzerland. Such a pure taste, I think. But I really am so sorry for you, Margaret.

Lady Windermere. [Smiling.] Why, Duchess?

Duchess of Berwick. Oh, on account of that horrid woman. She dresses so well, too, which makes it much worse, sets such a dreadful example. Augustus—you know my disreputable brother—such a trial to us all—well, Augustus is completely infatuated about her. It is quite scandalous, for she is absolutely inadmissible into society. Many a woman has a past, but I am told that she has at least a dozen, and that they all fit.

Lady Windermere. Whom are you talking about, Duchess?

Duchess of Berwick. About Mrs. Erlynne.

Lady Windermere. Mrs. Erlynne? I never heard of her, Duchess. And what has she to do with me?

Duchess of Berwick. My poor child! Agatha, darling!

Lady Agatha. Yes, mamma.

Duchess of Berwick. Will you go out on the terrace and look at the sunset?

Lady Agatha. Yes, mamma.

[Exit through window, L.]

Duchess of Berwick. Sweet girl! So devoted to sunsets! Shows such refinement of feeling, does it not? After all, there is nothing like Nature, is there?

Lady Windermere. But what is it, Duchess? Why do you talk to me about this person?

Duchess of Berwick. Don't you really know? I assure you we're all so distressed about it. Only last night at dear Lady Jansen's every one was saying how extraordinary it was that, of all men in London, Windermere should behave in such a way.

Lady Windermere. My husband—what has he got to do with any woman of that kind?

Duchess of Berwick. Ah, what indeed, dear? That is the point. He goes to see her continually, and stops for hours at a time, and while he is there she is not at home to any one. Not that many ladies call on her, dear, but she has a great many disreputable men friends—my own brother particularly, as I told you—and that is what makes it so dreadful about Windermere. We looked upon him as being such a model husband, but I am afraid there is no doubt about it. My dear nieces—you know the Saville girls, don't you?—such nice domestic creatures—plain, dreadfully plain, but so good—well, they're always at the window doing fancy work, and making ugly things for the poor, which I think so useful of them in these dreadful socialistic days, and this terrible woman has taken a house in Curzon Street, right opposite them—such a respectable street, too! I don't know what we're coming to! And they tell me that Windermere goes there four and five times a week—they see him. They can't help it—and although they never talk scandal, they—well, of course—they remark on it to every one. And the worst of it all is that I have been told that this woman has got a great deal of money out of somebody, for it seems that she came to London six months ago without anything at all to speak of, and now she has this charming house in Mayfair, drives her ponies in the Park every afternoon and all—well, all—since she has known poor dear Windermere.

Lady Windermere. Oh, I can't believe it!

Duchess of Berwick. But it's quite true, my dear. The whole of London knows it. That is why I felt it was better to come and talk to you, and advise you to take Windermere away at once to Homburg or to Aix, where he'll have something to amuse him, and where you can watch him all day long. I assure you, my dear, that on several occasions after I was first married, I had to pretend to be very ill, and was obliged to drink the most unpleasant mineral waters, merely to get Berwick out of town. He was so extremely susceptible. Though I am bound to say he never gave away any large sums of money to anybody. He is far too high-principled for that!

Lady Windermere. [Interrupting.] Duchess, Duchess, it's impossible! [Rising and crossing stage to C.] We are only married two years. Our child is but six months old. [Sits in chair R. of L. table.]

Duchess of Berwick. Ah, the dear pretty baby! How is the little darling? Is it a boy or a girl? I hope a girl—Ah, no, I remember it's a boy! I'm so sorry. Boys are so wicked. My boy is excessively immoral. You wouldn't believe at what hours he comes home. And he's only left Oxford a few months—I really don't know what they teach them there.

Lady Windermere. Are all men bad?

Duchess of Berwick. Oh, all of them, my dear, all of them, without any exception. And they never grow any better. Men become old, but they never become good.

Lady Windermere. Windermere and I married for love.

Duchess of Berwick. Yes, we begin like that. It was only Berwick's brutal and incessant threats of suicide that made me accept him at all, and before the year was out, he was running after all kinds of petticoats, every colour, every shape, every material. In fact, before the honeymoon was over, I caught him winking at my maid, a most pretty, respectable girl. I dismissed her at once without a character.—No, I remember I passed her on to my sister; poor dear Sir George is so short-sighted, I thought it wouldn't matter. But it did, though—it was most unfortunate. [Rises.] And now, my dear child, I must go, as we are dining out. And mind you don't take this little aberration of Windermere's too much to heart. Just take him abroad, and he'll come back to you all right.

Lady Windermere. Come back to me? [C.]

Duchess of Berwick. [L.C.] Yes, dear, these wicked women get our husbands away from us, but they always come back, slightly damaged, of course. And don't make scenes, men hate them!

Lady Windermere. It is very kind of you, Duchess, to come and tell me all this. But I can't believe that my husband is untrue to me.

Duchess of Berwick. Pretty child! I was like that once. Now I know that all men are monsters. [Lady Windermere rings bell.] The only thing to do is to feed the wretches well. A good cook does wonders, and that I know you have. My dear Margaret, you are not going to cry?

Lady Windermere. You needn't be afraid, Duchess, I never cry.

Duchess of Berwick. That's quite right, dear. Crying is the refuge of plain women but the ruin of pretty ones. Agatha, darling!

Lady Agatha. [Entering L.] Yes, mamma. [Stands back of table L.C.]

Duchess of Berwick. Come and bid good-bye to Lady Windermere, and thank her for your charming visit. [Coming down again.] And by the way, I must thank you for sending a card to Mr. Hopper—he's that rich young Australian people are taking such notice of just at present. His father made a great fortune by selling some kind of food in circular tins—most palatable, I believe—I fancy it is the thing the servants always refuse to eat. But the son is quite interesting. I think he's attracted by dear Agatha's clever talk. Of course, we should be very sorry to lose her, but I think that a mother who doesn't part with a daughter every season has no real affection. We're coming to-night, dear. [Parker opens C. doors.] And remember my advice, take the poor fellow out of town at once, it is the only thing to do. Good-bye, once more; come, Agatha.

[Exeunt Duchess and Lady Agatha C.]

Lady Windermere. How horrible! I understand now what Lord Darlington meant by the imaginary instance of the couple not two years married. Oh! it can't be true—she spoke of enormous sums of money paid to this woman. I know where Arthur keeps his bank book—in one of the drawers of that desk. I might find out by that. I will find out. [Opens drawer.] No, it is some hideous mistake. [Rises and goes C.] Some silly scandal! He loves me! He loves me! But why should I not look? I am his wife, I have a right to look! [Returns to bureau, takes out book and examines it page by page, smiles and gives a sigh of relief.] I knew it! there is not a word of truth in this stupid story. [Puts book back in drawer. As he does so, starts and takes out another book.] A second book—private—locked! [Tries to open it, but fails. Sees paper knife on bureau, and with it cuts cover from book. Begins to start at the first page.] 'Mrs. Erlynne—£600—Mrs. Erlynne—£700—Mrs. Erlynne—£400.' Oh! it is true! It is true! How horrible! [Throws book on floor.]

[Enter Lord Windermere C.]

Lord Windermere. Well, dear, has the fan been sent home yet? [Going R.C. Sees book.] Margaret, you have cut open my bank book. You have no right to do such a thing!

Lady Windermere. You think it wrong that you are found out, don't you?

Lord Windermere. I think it wrong that a wife should spy on her husband.

Lady Windermere. I did not spy on you. I never knew of this woman's existence till half an hour ago. Some one who pitied me was kind enough to tell me what every one in London knows already—your daily visits to Curzon Street, your mad infatuation, the monstrous sums of money you squander on this infamous woman! [Crossing L.]

Lord Windermere. Margaret! don't talk like that of Mrs. Erlynne, you don't know how unjust it is!

Lady Windermere. [Turning to him.] You are very jealous of Mrs. Erlynne's honour. I wish you had been as jealous of mine.

Lord Windermere. Your honour is untouched, Margaret. You don't think for a moment that—[Puts book back into desk.]

Lady Windermere. I think that you spend your money strangely. That is all. Oh, don't imagine I mind about the money. As far as I am concerned, you may squander everything we have. But what I do mind is that you who have loved me, you who have taught me to love you, should pass from the love that is given to the love that is bought. Oh, it's horrible! [Sits on sofa.] And it is I who feel degraded! you don't feel anything. I feel stained, utterly stained. You can't realise how hideous the last six months seems to me now—every kiss you have given me is tainted in my memory.

Lord Windermere. [Crossing to her.] Don't say that, Margaret. I never loved any one in the whole world but you.

Lady Windermere. [Rises.] Who is this woman, then? Why do you take a house for her?

Lord Windermere. I did not take a house for her.

Lady Windermere. You gave her the money to do it, which is the same thing.

Lord Windermere. Margaret, as far as I have known Mrs. Erlynne—

Lady Windermere. Is there a Mr. Erlynne—or is he a myth?

Lord Windermere. Her husband died many years ago. She is alone in the world.

Lady Windermere. No relations? [A pause.]

Lord Windermere. None.

Lady Windermere. Rather curious, isn't it? [L.]

Lord Windermere. [L.C.] Margaret, I was saying to you—and I beg you to listen to me—that as far as I have known Mrs. Erlynne, she has conducted herself well. If years ago—

Lady Windermere. Oh! [Crossing R.C.] I don't want details about her life!

Lord Windermere. [C.] I am not going to give you any details about her life. I tell you simply this—Mrs. Erlynne was once honoured, loved, respected. She was well born, she had position—she lost everything—threw it away, if you like. That makes it all the more bitter. Misfortunes one can endure—they come from outside, they are accidents. But to suffer for one's own faults—ah!—there is the sting of life. It was twenty years ago, too. She was little more than a girl then. She had been a wife for even less time than you have.

Lady Windermere. I am not interested in her—and—you should not mention this woman and me in the same breath. It is an error of taste. [Sitting R. at desk.]

Lord Windermere. Margaret, you could save this woman. She wants to get back into society, and she wants you to help her. [Crossing to her.]

Lady Windermere. Me!

Lord Windermere. Yes, you.

Lady Windermere. How impertinent of her! [A pause.]

Lord Windermere. Margaret, I came to ask you a great favour, and I still ask it of you, though you have discovered what I had intended you should never have known that I have given Mrs. Erlynne a large sum of money. I want you to send her an invitation for our party to-night. [Standing L. of her.]

Lady Windermere. You are mad! [Rises.]

Lord Windermere. I entreat you. People may chatter about her, do chatter about her, of course, but they don't know anything definite against her. She has been to several houses—not to houses where you would go, I admit, but still to houses where women who are in what is called Society nowadays do go. That does not content her. She wants you to receive her once.

Lady Windermere. As a triumph for her, I suppose?

Lord Windermere. No; but because she knows that you are a good woman—and that if she comes here once she will have a chance of a happier, a surer life than she has had. She will make no further effort to know you. Won't you help a woman who is trying to get back?

Lady Windermere. No! If a woman really repents, she never wishes to return to the society that has made or seen her ruin.

Lord Windermere. I beg of you.

Lady Windermere. [Crossing to door R.] I am going to dress for dinner, and don't mention the subject again this evening. Arthur [going to him C.], you fancy because I have no father or mother that I am alone in the world, and that you can treat me as you choose. You are wrong, I have friends, many friends.

Lord Windermere. [L.C.] Margaret, you are talking foolishly, recklessly. I won't argue with you, but I insist upon your asking Mrs. Erlynne to-night.

Lady Windermere. [R.C.] I shall do nothing of the kind. [Crossing L.C.]

Lord Windermere. You refuse? [C.]

Lady Windermere. Absolutely!

Lord Windermere. Ah, Margaret, do this for my sake; it is her last chance.

Lady Windermere. What has that to do with me?

Lord Windermere. How hard good women are!

Lady Windermere. How weak bad men are!

Lord Windermere. Margaret, none of us men may be good enough for the women we marry—that is quite true—but you don't imagine I would ever—oh, the suggestion is monstrous!

Lady Windermere. Why should you be different from other men? I am told that there is hardly a husband in London who does not waste his life over some shameful passion.

Lord Windermere. I am not one of them.

Lady Windermere. I am not sure of that!

Lord Windermere. You are sure in your heart. But don't make chasm after chasm between us. God knows the last few minutes have thrust us wide enough apart. Sit down and write the card.

Lady Windermere. Nothing in the whole world would induce me.

Lord Windermere. [Crossing to bureau.] Then I will! [Rings electric bell, sits and writes card.]

Lady Windermere. You are going to invite this woman? [Crossing to him.]

Lord Windermere. Yes. [Pause. Enter Parker.] Parker!

Parker. Yes, my lord. [Comes down L.C.]

Lord Windermere. Have this note sent to Mrs. Erlynne at No. 84A Curzon Street. [Crossing to L.C. and giving note to Parker.] There is no answer!

[Exit Parker C.]

Lady Windermere. Arthur, if that woman comes here, I shall insult her.

Lord Windermere. Margaret, don't say that.

Lady Windermere. I mean it.

Lord Windermere. Child, if you did such a thing, there's not a woman in London who wouldn't pity you.

Lady Windermere. There is not a good woman in London who would not applaud me. We have been too lax. We must make an example. I propose to begin to-night. [Picking up fan.] Yes, you gave me this fan to-day; it was your birthday present. If that woman crosses my threshold, I shall strike her across the face with it.

Lord Windermere. Margaret, you couldn't do such a thing.

Lady Windermere. You don't know me! [Moves R.]

[Enter Parker.]

Parker!

Parker. Yes, my lady.

Lady Windermere. I shall dine in my own room. I don't want dinner, in fact. See that everything is ready by half-past ten. And, Parker, be sure you pronounce the names of the guests very distinctly to-night. Sometimes you speak so fast that I miss them. I am particularly anxious to hear the names quite clearly, so as to make no mistake. You understand, Parker?

Parker. Yes, my lady.

Lady Windermere. That will do!

[Exit Parker C.]

[Speaking to Lord Windermere.] Arthur, if that woman comes here—I warn you—

Lord Windermere. Margaret, you'll ruin us!

Lady Windermere. Us! From this moment my life is separate from yours. But if you wish to avoid a public scandal, write at once to this woman, and tell her that I forbid her to come here!

Lord Windermere. I will not—I cannot—she must come!

Lady Windermere. Then I shall do exactly as I have said. [Goes R.] You leave me no choice.

[Exit R.]

Lord Windermere. [Calling after her.] Margaret! Margaret! [A pause.] My God! What shall I do? I dare not tell her who this woman really is. The shame would kill her. [Sinks down into a chair and buries his face in his hands.]

Act Drop

SECOND ACT

SCENE

Drawing-room in Lord Windermere's house. Door R.U. opening into ball-room, where band is playing. Door L. through which guests are entering. Door L.U. opens on to illuminated terrace. Palms, flowers, and brilliant lights. Room crowded with guests. Lady Windermere is receiving them.

Duchess of Berwick. [Up C.] So strange Lord Windermere isn't here. Mr. Hopper is very late, too. You have kept those five dances for him, Agatha? [Comes down.]

Lady Agatha. Yes, mamma.

Duchess of Berwick. [Sitting on sofa.] Just let me see your card. I'm so glad Lady Windermere has revived cards.—They're a mother's only safeguard. You dear simple little thing! [Scratches out two names.] No nice girl should ever waltz with such particularly younger sons! It looks so fast! The last two dances you might pass on the terrace with Mr. Hopper.

[Enter Mr. Dumby and Lady Plymdale from the ball-room.]

Lady Agatha. Yes, mamma.

Duchess of Berwick. [Fanning herself.] The air is so pleasant there.

Parker. Mrs. Cowper-Cowper. Lady Stutfield. Sir James Royston. Mr. Guy Berkeley.

[These people enter as announced.]

Dumby. Good evening, Lady Stutfield. I suppose this will be the last ball of the season?

Lady Stutfield. I suppose so, Mr. Dumby. It's been a delightful season, hasn't it?

Dumby. Quite delightful! Good evening, Duchess. I suppose this will be the last ball of the season?

Duchess of Berwick. I suppose so, Mr. Dumby. It has been a very dull season, hasn't it?

Dumby. Dreadfully dull! Dreadfully dull!

Mr. Cowper-Cowper. Good evening, Mr. Dumby. I suppose this will be the last ball of the season?

Dumby. Oh, I think not. There'll probably be two more. [Wanders back to Lady Plymdale.]

Parker. Mr. Rufford. Lady Jedburgh and Miss Graham. Mr. Hopper.

[These people enter as announced.]

Hopper. How do you do, Lady Windermere? How do you do, Duchess? [Bows to Lady Agatha.]

Duchess of Berwick. Dear Mr. Hopper, how nice of you to come so early. We all know how you are run after in London.

Hopper. Capital place, London! They are not nearly so exclusive in London as they are in Sydney.

Duchess of Berwick. Ah! we know your value, Mr. Hopper. We wish there were more like you. It would make life so much easier. Do you know, Mr. Hopper, dear Agatha and I are so much interested in Australia. It must be so pretty with all the dear little kangaroos flying about. Agatha has found it on the map. What a curious shape it is! Just like a large packing case. However, it is a very young country, isn't it?

Hopper. Wasn't it made at the same time as the others, Duchess?

Duchess of Berwick. How clever you are, Mr. Hopper. You have a cleverness quite of your own. Now I mustn't keep you.

Hopper. But I should like to dance with Lady Agatha, Duchess.

Duchess of Berwick. Well, I hope she has a dance left. Have you a dance left, Agatha?

Lady Agatha. Yes, mamma.

Duchess of Berwick. The next one?

Lady Agatha. Yes, mamma.

Hopper. May I have the pleasure? [Lady Agatha bows.]

Duchess of Berwick. Mind you take great care of my little chatterbox, Mr. Hopper.

[Lady Agatha and Mr. Hopper pass into ball-room.]

[Enter Lord Windermere.]

Lord Windermere. Margaret, I want to speak to you.

Lady Windermere. In a moment. [The music drops.]

Parker. Lord Augustus Lorton.

[Enter Lord Augustus.]

Lord Augustus. Good evening, Lady Windermere.

Duchess of Berwick. Sir James, will you take me into the ball-room? Augustus has been dining with us to-night. I really have had quite enough of dear Augustus for the moment.

[Sir James Royston gives the Duchess his arm and escorts her into the ball-room.]

Parker. Mr. and Mrs. Arthur Bowden. Lord and Lady Paisley. Lord Darlington.

[These people enter as announced.]

Lord Augustus. [Coming up to Lord Windermere.] Want to speak to you particularly, dear boy. I'm worn to a shadow. Know I don't look it. None of us men do look what we really are. Demmed good thing, too. What I want to know is this. Who is she? Where does she come from? Why hasn't she got any demmed relations? Demmed nuisance, relations! But they make one so demmed respectable.

Lord Windermere. You are talking of Mrs. Erlynne, I suppose? I only met her six months ago. Till then, I never knew of her existence.

Lord Augustus. You have seen a good deal of her since then.

Lord Windermere. [Coldly.] Yes, I have seen a good deal of her since then. I have just seen her.

Lord Augustus. Egad! the women are very down on her. I have been dining with Arabella this evening! By Jove! you should have heard what she said about Mrs. Erlynne. She didn't leave a rag on her. . . . [Aside.] Berwick and I told her that didn't matter much, as the lady in question must have an extremely fine figure. You should have seen Arabella's expression! . . . But, look here, dear boy. I don't know what to do about Mrs. Erlynne. Egad! I might be married to her; she treats me with such demmed indifference. She's deuced clever, too! She explains everything. Egad! she explains you. She has got any amount of explanations for you—and all of them different.

Lord Windermere. No explanations are necessary about my friendship with Mrs. Erlynne.

Lord Augustus. Hem! Well, look here, dear old fellow. Do you think she will ever get into this demmed thing called Society? Would you introduce her to your wife? No use beating about the confounded bush. Would you do that?

Lord Windermere. Mrs. Erlynne is coming here to-night.

Lord Augustus. Your wife has sent her a card?

Lord Windermere. Mrs. Erlynne has received a card.

Lord Augustus. Then she's all right, dear boy. But why didn't you tell me that before? It would have saved me a heap of worry and demmed misunderstandings!

[Lady Agatha and Mr. Hopper cross and exit on terrace L.U.E.]

Parker. Mr. Cecil Graham!

[Enter Mr. Cecil Graham.]

Cecil Graham. [Bows to Lady Windermere, passes over and shakes hands with Lord Windermere.] Good evening, Arthur. Why don't you ask me how I am? I like people to ask me how I am. It shows a wide-spread interest in my health. Now, to-night I am not at all well. Been dining with my people. Wonder why it is one's people are always so tedious? My father would talk morality after dinner. I told him he was old enough to know better. But my experience is that as soon as people are old enough to know better, they don't know anything at all. Hallo, Tuppy! Hear you're going to be married again; thought you were tired of that game.

Lord Augustus. You're excessively trivial, my dear boy, excessively trivial!

Cecil Graham. By the way, Tuppy, which is it? Have you been twice married and once divorced, or twice divorced and once married? I say you've been twice divorced and once married. It seems so much more probable.

Lord Augustus. I have a very bad memory. I really don't remember which. [Moves away R.]

Lady Plymdale. Lord Windermere, I've something most particular to ask you.

Lord Windermere. I am afraid—if you will excuse me—I must join my wife.

Lady Plymdale. Oh, you mustn't dream of such a thing. It's most dangerous nowadays for a husband to pay any attention to his wife in public. It always makes people think that he beats her when they're alone. The world has grown so suspicious of anything that looks like a happy married life. But I'll tell you what it is at supper. [Moves towards door of ball-room.]

Lord Windermere. [C.] Margaret! I must speak to you.

Lady Windermere. Will you hold my fan for me, Lord Darlington? Thanks. [Comes down to him.]

Lord Windermere. [Crossing to her.] Margaret, what you said before dinner was, of course, impossible?

Lady Windermere. That woman is not coming here to-night!

Lord Windermere. [R.C.] Mrs. Erlynne is coming here, and if you in any way annoy or wound her, you will bring shame and sorrow on us both. Remember that! Ah, Margaret! only trust me! A wife should trust her husband!

Lady Windermere. [C.] London is full of women who trust their husbands. One can always recognise them. They look so thoroughly unhappy. I am not going to be one of them. [Moves up.] Lord Darlington, will you give me back my fan, please? Thanks. . . . A useful thing a fan, isn't it? . . . I want a friend to-night, Lord Darlington: I didn't know I would want one so soon.

Lord Darlington. Lady Windermere! I knew the time would come some day; but why to-night?

Lord Windermere. I will tell her. I must. It would be terrible if there were any scene. Margaret . . .

Parker. Mrs. Erlynne!

[Lord Windermere starts. Mrs. Erlynne enters, very beautifully dressed and very dignified. Lady Windermere clutches at her fan, then lets it drop on the door. She bows coldly to Mrs. Erlynne, who bows to her sweetly in turn, and sails into the room.]

Lord Darlington. You have dropped your fan, Lady Windermere. [Picks it up and hands it to her.]

Mrs. Erlynne. [C.] How do you do, again, Lord Windermere? How charming your sweet wife looks! Quite a picture!

Lord Windermere. [In a low voice.] It was terribly rash of you to come!

Mrs. Erlynne. [Smiling.] The wisest thing I ever did in my life. And, by the way, you must pay me a good deal of attention this evening. I am afraid of the women. You must introduce me to some of them. The men I can always manage. How do you do, Lord Augustus? You have quite neglected me lately. I have not seen you since yesterday. I am afraid you're faithless. Every one told me so.

Lord Augustus. [R.] Now really, Mrs. Erlynne, allow me to explain.

Mrs. Erlynne. [R.C.] No, dear Lord Augustus, you can't explain anything. It is your chief charm.

Lord Augustus. Ah! if you find charms in me, Mrs. Erlynne—

[They converse together. Lord Windermere moves uneasily about the room watching Mrs. Erlynne.]

Lord Darlington. [To Lady Windermere.] How pale you are!

Lady Windermere. Cowards are always pale!

Lord Darlington. You look faint. Come out on the terrace.

Lady Windermere. Yes. [To Parker.] Parker, send my cloak out.

Mrs. Erlynne. [Crossing to her.] Lady Windermere, how beautifully your terrace is illuminated. Reminds me of Prince Doria's at Rome.

[Lady Windermere bows coldly, and goes off with Lord Darlington.]

Oh, how do you do, Mr. Graham? Isn't that your aunt, Lady Jedburgh? I should so much like to know her.

Cecil Graham. [After a moment's hesitation and embarrassment.] Oh, certainly, if you wish it. Aunt Caroline, allow me to introduce Mrs. Erlynne.

Mrs. Erlynne. So pleased to meet you, Lady Jedburgh. [Sits beside her on the sofa.] Your nephew and I are great friends. I am so much interested in his political career. I think he's sure to be a wonderful success. He thinks like a Tory, and talks like a Radical, and that's so important nowadays. He's such a brilliant talker, too. But we all know from whom he inherits that. Lord Allandale was saying to me only yesterday, in the Park, that Mr. Graham talks almost as well as his aunt.

Lady Jedburgh. [R.] Most kind of you to say these charming things to me! [Mrs. Erlynne smiles, and continues conversation.]

Dumby. [To Cecil Graham.] Did you introduce Mrs. Erlynne to Lady Jedburgh?

Cecil Graham. Had to, my dear fellow. Couldn't help it! That woman can make one do anything she wants. How, I don't know.

Dumby. Hope to goodness she won't speak to me! [Saunters towards Lady Plymdale.]

Mrs. Erlynne. [C. To Lady Jedburgh.] On Thursday? With great pleasure. [Rises, and speaks to Lord Windermere, laughing.] What a bore it is to have to be civil to these old dowagers! But they always insist on it!

Lady Plymdale. [To Mr. Dumby.] Who is that well-dressed woman talking to Windermere?

Dumby. Haven't got the slightest idea! Looks like an édition de luxe of a wicked French novel, meant specially for the English market.

Mrs. Erlynne. So that is poor Dumby with Lady Plymdale? I hear she is frightfully jealous of him. He doesn't seem anxious to speak to me to-night. I suppose he is afraid of her. Those straw-coloured women have dreadful tempers. Do you know, I think I'll dance with you first, Windermere. [Lord Windermere bites his lip and frowns.] It will make Lord Augustus so jealous! Lord Augustus! [Lord Augustus comes down.] Lord Windermere insists on my dancing with him first, and, as it's his own house, I can't well refuse. You know I would much sooner dance with you.

Lord Augustus. [With a low bow.] I wish I could think so, Mrs. Erlynne.

Mrs. Erlynne. You know it far too well. I can fancy a person dancing through life with you and finding it charming.

Lord Augustus. [Placing his hand on his white waistcoat.] Oh, thank you, thank you. You are the most adorable of all ladies!

Mrs. Erlynne. What a nice speech! So simple and so sincere! Just the sort of speech I like. Well, you shall hold my bouquet. [Goes towards ball-room on Lord Windermere's arm.] Ah, Mr. Dumby, how are you? I am so sorry I have been out the last three times you have called. Come and lunch on Friday.

Dumby. [With perfect nonchalance.] Delighted!

[Lady Plymdale glares with indignation at Mr. Dumby. Lord Augustus follows Mrs. Erlynne and Lord Windermere into the ball-room holding bouquet.]

Lady Plymdale. [To Mr. Dumby.] What an absolute brute you are! I never can believe a word you say! Why did you tell me you didn't know her? What do you mean by calling on her three times running? You are not to go to lunch there; of course you understand that?

Dumby. My dear Laura, I wouldn't dream of going!

Lady Plymdale. You haven't told me her name yet! Who is she?

Dumby. [Coughs slightly and smooths his hair.] She's a Mrs. Erlynne.

Lady Plymdale. That woman!

Dumby. Yes; that is what every one calls her.

Lady Plymdale. How very interesting! How intensely interesting! I really must have a good stare at her. [Goes to door of ball-room and looks in.] I have heard the most shocking things about her. They say she is ruining poor Windermere. And Lady Windermere, who goes in for being so proper, invites her! How extremely amusing! It takes a thoroughly good woman to do a thoroughly stupid thing. You are to lunch there on Friday!

Dumby. Why?

Lady Plymdale. Because I want you to take my husband with you. He has been so attentive lately, that he has become a perfect nuisance. Now, this woman is just the thing for him. He'll dance attendance upon her as long as she lets him, and won't bother me. I assure you, women of that kind are most useful. They form the basis of other people's marriages.

Dumby. What a mystery you are!

Lady Plymdale. [Looking at him.] I wish you were!

Dumby. I am—to myself. I am the only person in the world I

should like to know thoroughly; but I don't see any chance of it just at present.

[They pass into the ball-room, and Lady Windermere and Lord Darlington enter from the terrace.]

Lady Windermere. Yes. Her coming here is monstrous, unbearable. I know now what you meant to-day at tea-time. Why didn't you tell me right out? You should have!

Lord Darlington. I couldn't! A man can't tell these things about another man! But if I had known he was going to make you ask her here to-night, I think I would have told you. That insult, at any rate, you would have been spared.

Lady Windermere. I did not ask her. He insisted on her coming—against my entreaties—against my commands. Oh! the house is tainted for me! I feel that every woman here sneers at me as she dances by with my husband. What have I done to deserve this? I gave him all my life. He took it—used it—spoiled it! I am degraded in my own eyes; and I lack courage—I am a coward! [Sits down on sofa.]

Lord Darlington. If I know you at all, I know that you can't live with a man who treats you like this! What sort of life would you have with him? You would feel that he was lying to you every moment of the day. You would feel that the look in his eyes was false, his voice false, his touch false, his passion false. He would come to you when he was weary of others; you would have to comfort him. He would come to you when he was devoted to others; you would have to charm him. You would have to be to him the mask of his real life, the cloak to hide his secret.

Lady Windermere. You are right—you are terribly right. But where am I to turn? You said you would be my friend, Lord Darlington.—Tell me, what am I to do? Be my friend now.

Lord Darlington. Between men and women there is no friendship possible. There is passion, enmity, worship, love, but no friendship. I love you—

Lady Windermere. No, no! [Rises.]

Lord Darlington. Yes, I love you! You are more to me than anything in the whole world. What does your husband give you? Nothing. Whatever is in him he gives to this wretched woman, whom he has thrust into your society, into your home, to shame you before every one. I offer you my life—

Lady Windermere. Lord Darlington!

Lord Darlington. My life—my whole life. Take it, and do with it what you will. . . . I love you—love you as I have never loved any living thing. From the moment I met you I loved you, loved you blindly, adoringly, madly! You did not know it then—you know it now! Leave this house to-night. I won't tell you that the world matters nothing, or the world's voice, or the voice of society. They matter a great deal. They matter far too much. But there are moments when one has to choose between living one's own life, fully, entirely, completely—or dragging out some false, shallow, degrading existence that the world in its hypocrisy demands. You have that moment now. Choose! Oh, my love, choose.

Lady Windermere. [Moving slowly away from him, and looking at him with startled eyes.] I have not the courage.

Lord Darlington. [Following her.] Yes; you have the courage. There may be six months of pain, of disgrace even, but when you no longer bear his name, when you bear mine, all will be well. Margaret, my love, my wife that shall be some day—yes, my wife! You know it! What are you now? This woman has the place that belongs by right to you. Oh! go—go out of this house, with head erect, with a smile upon your lips, with courage in your eyes. All London will know why you did it; and who will blame you? No one. If they do, what matter? Wrong? What is wrong? It's wrong for a man to abandon his wife for a shameless woman. It is wrong for a wife to remain with a man who so dishonours her. You said once you would make no compromise with things. Make none now. Be brave! Be yourself!

Lady Windermere. I am afraid of being myself. Let me think! Let me wait! My husband may return to me. [Sits down on sofa.]

Lord Darlington. And you would take him back! You are not what I thought you were. You are just the same as every other woman. You would stand anything rather than face the censure of a world, whose praise you would despise. In a week you will be driving with this woman in the Park. She will be your constant guest—your dearest friend. You would endure anything rather than break with one blow this monstrous tie. You are right. You have no courage; none!

Lady Windermere. Ah, give me time to think. I cannot answer you now. [Passes her hand nervously over her brow.]

Lord Darlington. It must be now or not at all.

Lady Windermere. [Rising from the sofa.] Then, not at all! [A pause.]

Lord Darlington. You break my heart!

Lady Windermere. Mine is already broken. [A pause.]

Lord Darlington. To-morrow I leave England. This is the last time I shall ever look on you. You will never see me again. For one moment our lives met—our souls touched. They must never meet or touch again. Good-bye, Margaret. [Exit.]

Lady Windermere. How alone I am in life! How terribly alone!

[The music stops. Enter the Duchess of Berwick and Lord Paisley laughing and talking. Other guests come on from ball-room.]

Duchess of Berwick. Dear Margaret, I've just been having such a delightful chat with Mrs. Erlynne. I am so sorry for what I said to you this afternoon about her. Of course, she must be all right if you invite her. A most attractive woman, and has such sensible views on life. Told me she entirely disapproved of people marrying more than once, so I feel quite safe about poor Augustus. Can't imagine why people speak against her. It's those horrid nieces of mine—the Saville girls—they're always talking scandal. Still, I should go to Homburg, dear, I really should. She is just a little too attractive. But where is Agatha? Oh, there she is: [Lady Agatha and Mr. Hopper enter from terrace L.U.E.] Mr. Hopper, I am very, very angry with you. You have taken Agatha out on the terrace, and she is so delicate.

Hopper. Awfully sorry, Duchess. We went out for a moment and then got chatting together.

Duchess of Berwick. [C.] Ah, about dear Australia, I suppose?

Hopper. Yes!

Duchess of Berwick. Agatha, darling! [Beckons her over.]

Lady Agatha. Yes, mamma!

Duchess of Berwick. [Aside.] Did Mr. Hopper definitely—

Lady Agatha. Yes, mamma.

Duchess of Berwick. And what answer did you give him, dear child?

Lady Agatha. Yes, mamma.

Duchess of Berwick. [Affectionately.] My dear one! You always say the right thing. Mr. Hopper! James! Agatha has told me everything. How cleverly you have both kept your secret.

Hopper. You don't mind my taking Agatha off to Australia, then, Duchess?

Duchess of Berwick. [Indignantly.] To Australia? Oh, don't mention that dreadful vulgar place.

Hopper. But she said she'd like to come with me.

Duchess of Berwick. [Severely.] Did you say that, Agatha?

Lady Agatha. Yes, mamma.

Duchess of Berwick. Agatha, you say the most silly things possible. I think on the whole that Grosvenor Square would be a more healthy place to reside in. There are lots of vulgar people live in Grosvenor Square, but at any rate there are no horrid kangaroos crawling about. But we'll talk about that to-morrow. James, you can take Agatha down. You'll come to lunch, of course, James. At half-past one, instead of two. The Duke will wish to say a few words to you, I am sure.

Hopper. I should like to have a chat with the Duke, Duchess. He has not said a single word to me yet.

Duchess of Berwick. I think you'll find he will have a great deal to say to you to-morrow. [Exit Lady Agatha with Mr. Hopper.] And now good-night, Margaret. I'm afraid it's the old, old story, dear. Love—well, not love at first sight, but love at the end of the season, which is so much more satisfactory.

Lady Windermere. Good-night, Duchess.

[Exit the Duchess of Berwick on Lord Paisley's arm.]

Lady Plymdale. My dear Margaret, what a handsome woman your husband has been dancing with! I should be quite jealous if I were you! Is she a great friend of yours?

Lady Windermere. No!

Lady Plymdale. Really? Good-night, dear. [Looks at Mr. Dumby and exit.]

Dumby. Awful manners young Hopper has!

Cecil Graham. Ah! Hopper is one of Nature's gentlemen, the worst type of gentleman I know.

Dumby. Sensible woman, Lady Windermere. Lots of wives would have objected to Mrs. Erlynne coming. But Lady Windermere has that uncommon thing called common sense.

Cecil Graham. And Windermere knows that nothing looks so like innocence as an indiscretion.

Dumby. Yes; dear Windermere is becoming almost modern. Never thought he would. [Bows to Lady Windermere and exit.]

Lady Jedburgh. Good night, Lady Windermere. What a fascinating woman Mrs. Erlynne is! She is coming to lunch on Thursday, won't you come too? I expect the Bishop and dear Lady Merton.

Lady Windermere. I am afraid I am engaged, Lady Jedburgh.

Lady Jedburgh. So sorry. Come, dear. [Exeunt Lady Jedburgh and Miss Graham.]

[Enter Mrs. Erlynne and Lord Windermere.]

Mrs. Erlynne. Charming ball it has been! Quite reminds me of old days. [Sits on sofa.] And I see that there are just as many fools in society as there used to be. So pleased to find that nothing has altered! Except Margaret. She's grown quite pretty. The last time I saw her—twenty years ago, she was a fright in flannel. Positive fright, I assure you. The dear Duchess! and that sweet Lady Agatha! Just the type of girl I like! Well, really, Windermere, if I am to be the Duchess's sister-in-law—

Lord Windermere. [Sitting L. of her.] But are you—?

[Exit Mr. Cecil Graham with rest of guests. Lady Windermere watches, with a look of scorn and pain, Mrs. Erlynne and her husband. They are unconscious of her presence.]

Mrs. Erlynne. Oh, yes! He's to call to-morrow at twelve o'clock! He wanted to propose to-night. In fact he did. He kept on proposing. Poor Augustus, you know how he repeats himself. Such a bad habit! But I told him I wouldn't give him an answer till to-morrow. Of course I am going to take him. And I dare say I'll make him an admirable wife, as wives go. And there is a great deal of good in Lord Augustus. Fortunately it is all on the surface. Just where good qualities should be. Of course you must help me in this matter.

Lord Windermere. I am not called on to encourage Lord Augustus, I suppose?

Mrs. Erlynne. Oh, no! I do the encouraging. But you will make me a handsome settlement, Windermere, won't you?

Lord Windermere. [Frowning.] Is that what you want to talk to me about to-night?

Mrs. Erlynne. Yes.

Lord Windermere. [With a gesture of impatience.] I will not talk of it here.

Mrs. Erlynne. [Laughing.] Then we will talk of it on the terrace. Even business should have a picturesque background. Should it not, Windermere? With a proper background women can do anything.

Lord Windermere. Won't to-morrow do as well?

Mrs. Erlynne. No; you see, to-morrow I am going to accept him. And I think it would be a good thing if I was able to tell him that I had—well, what shall I say?—£2000 a year left to me by a third cousin—or a second husband—or some distant relative of that kind. It would be an additional attraction, wouldn't it? You have a delightful opportunity now of paying me a compliment, Windermere. But you are not very clever at paying compliments. I am afraid Margaret doesn't encourage you in that excellent habit. It's a great mistake on her part. When men give up saying what is charming, they give up thinking what is charming. But seriously, what do you say to £2000? £2500, I think. In modern life margin is everything. Windermere, don't you think the world an intensely amusing place? I do!

[Exit on terrace with Lord Windermere. Music strikes up in ball-room.]

Lady Windermere. To stay in this house any longer is impossible. To-night a man who loves me offered me his whole life. I refused it. It was foolish of me. I will offer him mine now. I will give him mine. I will go to him! [Puts on cloak and goes to the door, then turns back. Sits down at table and writes a letter, puts it into an envelope, and leaves it on table.] Arthur has never understood me. When he reads this, he will. He may do as he chooses now with his life. I have done with mine as I think best, as I think right. It is he who has broken the bond of marriage—not I. I only break its bondage.

[Exit.]

[Parker enters L. and crosses towards the ball-room R. Enter Mrs. Erlynne.]

Mrs. Erlynne. Is Lady Windermere in the ball-room?

Parker. Her ladyship has just gone out.

Mrs. Erlynne. Gone out? She's not on the terrace?

Parker. No, madam. Her ladyship has just gone out of the house.

Mrs. Erlynne. [Starts, and looks at the servant with a puzzled expression in her face.] Out of the house?

Parker. Yes, madam—her ladyship told me she had left a letter for his lordship on the table.

Mrs. Erlynne. A letter for Lord Windermere?

Parker. Yes, madam.

Mrs. Erlynne. Thank you.

[Exit Parker. The music in the ball-room stops.] Gone out of her house! A letter addressed to her husband! [Goes over to bureau and looks at letter. Takes it up and lays it down again with a shudder of fear.] No, no! It would be impossible! Life doesn't repeat its tragedies like that! Oh, why does this horrible fancy come across me? Why do I remember now the one moment of my life I most wish to forget? Does life repeat its tragedies? [Tears letter open and reads it, then sinks down into a chair with a gesture of anguish.] Oh, how terrible! The same words that twenty years ago I wrote to her father! and how bitterly I have been punished for it! No; my punishment, my real punishment is to-night, is now! [Still seated R.]

[Enter Lord Windermere L.U.E.]

Lord Windermere. Have you said good-night to my wife? [Comes C.]

Mrs. Erlynne. [Crushing letter in her hand.] Yes.

Lord Windermere. Where is she?

Mrs. Erlynne. She is very tired. She has gone to bed. She said she had a headache.

Lord Windermere. I must go to her. You'll excuse me?

Mrs. Erlynne. [Rising hurriedly.] Oh, no! It's nothing serious. She's only very tired, that is all. Besides, there are people still in the supper-room. She wants you to make her apologies to them. She said she didn't wish to be disturbed. [Drops letter.] She asked me to tell you!

Lord Windermere. [Picks up letter.] You have dropped something.

Mrs. Erlynne. Oh yes, thank you, that is mine. [Puts out her hand to take it.]

Lord Windermere. [Still looking at letter.] But it's my wife's handwriting, isn't it?

Mrs. Erlynne. [Takes the letter quickly.] Yes, it's—an address. Will you ask them to call my carriage, please?

Lord Windermere. Certainly.

[Goes L. and Exit.]

Mrs. Erlynne. Thanks! What can I do? What can I do? I feel a passion awakening within me that I never felt before. What can it mean? The daughter must not be like the mother—that would be terrible. How can I save her? How can I save my child? A moment may ruin a life. Who knows that better than I? Windermere must be got out of the house; that is absolutely necessary. [Goes L.] But how shall I do it? It must be done somehow. Ah!

[Enter Lord Augustus R.U.E. carrying bouquet.]

Lord Augustus. Dear lady, I am in such suspense! May I not have an answer to my request?

Mrs. Erlynne. Lord Augustus, listen to me. You are to take Lord Windermere down to your club at once, and keep him there as long as possible. You understand?

Lord Augustus. But you said you wished me to keep early hours!

Mrs. Erlynne. [Nervously.] Do what I tell you. Do what I tell you.

Lord Augustus. And my reward?

Mrs. Erlynne. Your reward? Your reward? Oh! ask me that to-morrow. But don't let Windermere out of your sight to-night. If you do I will never forgive you. I will never speak to you again. I'll have nothing to do with you. Remember you are to keep Windermere at your club, and don't let him come back to-night.

[Exit L.]

Lord Augustus. Well, really, I might be her husband already. Positively I might. [Follows her in a bewildered manner.]

Act Drop.

THIRD ACT

SCENE

Lord Darlington's Rooms. A large sofa is in front of fireplace R. At the back of the stage a curtain is drawn across the window. Doors L. and R. Table R. with writing materials. Table C. with syphons, glasses, and Tantalus frame. Table L. with cigar and cigarette box. Lamps lit.

Lady Windermere. [Standing by the fireplace.] Why doesn't he come? This waiting is horrible. He should be here. Why is he not here, to wake by passionate words some fire within me? I am cold—cold as a loveless thing. Arthur must have read my letter by this time. If he cared for me, he would have come after me, would have taken me back by force. But he doesn't care. He's entrammelled by this woman—fascinated by her—dominated by her. If a woman wants to hold a man, she has merely to appeal to what is worst in him. We make gods of men and they leave us. Others make brutes of them and they fawn and are faithful. How hideous life is! . . . Oh! it was mad of me to come here, horribly mad. And yet, which is the worst, I wonder, to be at the mercy of a man who loves one, or the wife of a man who in one's own house dishonours one? What woman knows? What woman in the whole world? But will he love me always, this man to whom I am giving my life? What do I bring him? Lips that have lost the note of joy, eyes that are blinded by tears, chill hands and icy heart. I bring him nothing. I must go back—no; I can't go back, my letter has put me in their power—Arthur would not take me back! That fatal letter! No! Lord Darlington leaves England to-morrow. I will go with him—I have no choice. [Sits down for a few moments. Then starts up and puts on her cloak.] No, no! I will go back, let Arthur do with me what he pleases. I can't wait here. It has been madness my coming. I must go at once. As for Lord Darlington—Oh! here he is! What shall I do? What can I say to him? Will he let me go away at all? I have heard that men are brutal, horrible . . . Oh! [Hides her face in her hands.]

[Enter Mrs. Erlynne L.]

Mrs. Erlynne. Lady Windermere! [Lady Windermere starts and looks up. Then recoils in contempt.] Thank Heaven I am in time. You must go back to your husband's house immediately.

Lady Windermere. Must?

Mrs. Erlynne. [Authoritatively.] Yes, you must! There is not a second to be lost. Lord Darlington may return at any moment.

Lady Windermere. Don't come near me!

Mrs. Erlynne. Oh! You are on the brink of ruin, you are on the brink of a hideous precipice. You must leave this place at once, my carriage is waiting at the corner of the street. You must come with me and drive straight home.

[Lady Windermere throws off her cloak and flings it on the sofa.]

What are you doing?

Lady Windermere. Mrs. Erlynne—if you had not come here, I would have gone back. But now that I see you, I feel that nothing in the whole world would induce me to live under the same roof as Lord Windermere. You fill me with horror. There is something about you that stirs the wildest—rage within me. And I know why you are here. My husband sent you to lure me back that I might serve as a blind to whatever relations exist between you and him.

Mrs. Erlynne. Oh! You don't think that—you can't.

Lady Windermere. Go back to my husband, Mrs. Erlynne. He belongs to you and not to me. I suppose he is afraid of a scandal. Men are such cowards. They outrage every law of the world, and are afraid of the world's tongue. But he had better prepare himself. He shall have a scandal. He shall have the worst scandal there has been in London for years. He shall see his name in every vile paper, mine on every hideous placard.

Mrs. Erlynne. No—no—

Lady Windermere. Yes! he shall. Had he come himself, I admit I would have gone back to the life of degradation you and he had prepared for me—I was going back—but to stay himself at home, and to send you as his messenger—oh! it was infamous—infamous.

Mrs. Erlynne. [C.] Lady Windermere, you wrong me horribly—you wrong your husband horribly. He doesn't know you are here—he thinks you are safe in your own house. He thinks you are asleep in your own room. He never read the mad letter you wrote to him!

Lady Windermere. [R.] Never read it!

Mrs. Erlynne. No—he knows nothing about it.

Lady Windermere. How simple you think me! [Going to her.] You are lying to me!

Mrs. Erlynne. [Restraining herself.] I am not. I am telling you the truth.

Lady Windermere. If my husband didn't read my letter, how is it that you are here? Who told you I had left the house you were shameless enough to enter? Who told you where I had gone to? My husband told you, and sent you to decoy me back. [Crosses L.]

Mrs. Erlynne. [R.C.] Your husband has never seen the letter. I—saw it, I opened it. I—read it.

Lady Windermere. [Turning to her.] You opened a letter of mine to my husband? You wouldn't dare!

Mrs. Erlynne. Dare! Oh! to save you from the abyss into which you are falling, there is nothing in the world I would not dare, nothing in the whole world. Here is the letter. Your husband has never read it. He never shall read it. [Going to fireplace.] It should never have been written. [Tears it and throws it into the fire.]

Lady Windermere. [With infinite contempt in her voice and look.] How do I know that that was my letter after all? You seem to think the commonest device can take me in!

Mrs. Erlynne. Oh! why do you disbelieve everything I tell you? What object do you think I have in coming here, except to save you from utter ruin, to save you from the consequence of a hideous mistake? That letter that is burnt now was your letter. I swear it to you!

Lady Windermere. [Slowly.] You took good care to burn it before I had examined it. I cannot trust you. You, whose whole life is a lie, could you speak the truth about anything? [Sits down.]

Mrs. Erlynne. [Hurriedly.] Think as you like about me—say what you choose against me, but go back, go back to the husband you love.

Lady Windermere. [Sullenly.] I do not love him!

Mrs. Erlynne. You do, and you know that he loves you.

Lady Windermere. He does not understand what love is. He understands it as little as you do—but I see what you want. It would be a great advantage for you to get me back. Dear Heaven! what a life I would have then! Living at the mercy of a woman who has neither mercy nor pity in her, a woman whom it is an infamy to meet, a degradation to know, a vile woman, a woman who comes between husband and wife!

Mrs. Erlynne. [With a gesture of despair.] Lady Windermere, Lady Windermere, don't say such terrible things. You don't know how terrible they are, how terrible and how unjust. Listen, you must listen! Only go back to your husband, and I promise you never to communicate with him again on any pretext—never to see him—never to have anything to do with his life or yours.

The money that he gave me, he gave me not through love, but through hatred, not in worship, but in contempt. The hold I have over him—

Lady Windermere. [Rising.] Ah! you admit you have a hold!

Mrs. Erlynne. Yes, and I will tell you what it is. It is his love for you, Lady Windermere.

Lady Windermere. You expect me to believe that?

Mrs. Erlynne. You must believe it! It is true. It is his love for you that has made him submit to—oh! call it what you like, tyranny, threats, anything you choose. But it is his love for you. His desire to spare you—shame, yes, shame and disgrace.

Lady Windermere. What do you mean? You are insolent! What have I to do with you?

Mrs. Erlynne. [Humbly.] Nothing. I know it—but I tell you that your husband loves you—that you may never meet with such love again in your whole life—that such love you will never meet—and that if you throw it away, the day may come when you will starve for love and it will not be given to you, beg for love and it will be denied you—Oh! Arthur loves you!

Lady Windermere. Arthur? And you tell me there is nothing between you?

Mrs. Erlynne. Lady Windermere, before Heaven your husband is guiltless of all offence towards you! And I—I tell you that had it ever occurred to me that such a monstrous suspicion would have entered your mind, I would have died rather than have crossed your life or his—oh! died, gladly died! [Moves away to sofa R.]

Lady Windermere. You talk as if you had a heart. Women like you have no hearts. Heart is not in you. You are bought and sold. [Sits L.C.]

Mrs. Erlynne. [Starts, with a gesture of pain. Then restrains herself, and comes over to where Lady Windermere is sitting. As she speaks, she stretches out her hands towards her, but does not dare to touch her.] Believe what you choose about me. I am not worth a moment's sorrow. But don't spoil your beautiful young life on my account! You don't know what may be in store for you, unless you leave this house at once. You don't know what it is to fall into the pit, to be despised, mocked, abandoned, sneered at—to be an outcast! to find the door shut against one, to have to creep in by hideous byways, afraid every moment lest the mask should be stripped from one's face, and all the while to hear the laughter, the horrible laughter of the world, a thing more tragic than all the tears the world has ever shed. You don't know what it is. One pays for one's sin, and then one pays again, and all one's life one pays. You must never know that.—As for me, if suffering be an expiation, then at this moment I have expiated all my faults, whatever they have been; for to-night you have made a heart in one who had it not, made it and broken it.—But let that pass. I may have wrecked my own life, but I will not let you wreck yours. You—why, you are a mere girl, you would be lost. You haven't got the kind of brains that enables a woman to get back. You have neither the wit nor the courage. You couldn't stand dishonour! No! Go back, Lady Windermere, to the husband who loves you, whom you love. You have a child, Lady Windermere. Go back to that child who even now, in pain or in joy, may be calling to you. [Lady Windermere rises.] God gave you that child. He will require from you that you make his life fine, that you watch over him. What answer will you make to God if his life is ruined through you? Back to your house, Lady Windermere—your husband loves you! He has never swerved for a moment from the love he bears you. But even if he had a thousand loves, you must stay with your child. If he was harsh to you, you must stay with your child. If he ill-treated you, you must stay with your child. If he abandoned you, your place is with your child.

[Lady Windermere bursts into tears and buries her face in her hands.]

[Rushing to her.] Lady Windermere!

Lady Windermere. [Holding out her hands to her, helplessly, as a child might do.] Take me home. Take me home.

Mrs. Erlynne. [Is about to embrace her. Then restrains herself. There is a look of wonderful joy in her face.] Come! Where is your cloak? [Getting it from sofa.] Here. Put it on. Come at once!

[They go to the door.]

Lady Windermere. Stop! Don't you hear voices?

Mrs. Erlynne. No, no! There was no one!

Lady Windermere. Yes, there is! Listen! Oh! that is my husband's voice! He is coming in! Save me! Oh, it's some plot! You have sent for him.

[Voices outside.]

Mrs. Erlynne. Silence! I'm here to save you, if I can. But I fear it is too late! There! [Points to the curtain across the window.] The first chance you have, slip out, if you ever get a chance!

Lady Windermere. But you?

Mrs. Erlynne. Oh! never mind me. I'll face them.

[Lady Windermere hides herself behind the curtain.]

Lord Augustus. [Outside.] Nonsense, dear Windermere, you must not leave me!

Mrs. Erlynne. Lord Augustus! Then it is I who am lost! [Hesitates for a moment, then looks round and sees door R., and exits through it.]

[Enter Lord Darlington, Mr. Dumby, Lord Windermere, Lord Augustus Lorton, and Mr. Cecil Graham.

Dumby. What a nuisance their turning us out of the club at this hour! It's only two o'clock. [Sinks into a chair.] The lively part of the evening is only just beginning. [Yawns and closes his eyes.]

Lord Windermere. It is very good of you, Lord Darlington, allowing Augustus to force our company on you, but I'm afraid I can't stay long.

Lord Darlington. Really! I am so sorry! You'll take a cigar, won't you?

Lord Windermere. Thanks! [Sits down.]

Lord Augustus. [To Lord Windermere.] My dear boy, you must not dream of going. I have a great deal to talk to you about, of demmed importance, too. [Sits down with him at L. table.]

Cecil Graham. Oh! We all know what that is! Tuppy can't talk about anything but Mrs. Erlynne.

Lord Windermere. Well, that is no business of yours, is it, Cecil?

Cecil Graham. None! That is why it interests me. My own business always bores me to death. I prefer other people's.

Lord Darlington. Have something to drink, you fellows. Cecil, you'll have a whisky and soda?

Cecil Graham. Thanks. [Goes to table with Lord Darlington.] Mrs. Erlynne looked very handsome to-night, didn't she?

Lord Darlington. I am not one of her admirers.

Cecil Graham. I usen't to be, but I am now. Why! she actually made me introduce her to poor dear Aunt Caroline. I believe she is going to lunch there.

Lord Darlington. [In Purple.] No?

Cecil Graham. She is, really.

Lord Darlington. Excuse me, you fellows. I'm going away to-morrow. And I have to write a few letters. [Goes to writing table and sits down.]

Dumby. Clever woman, Mrs. Erlynne.

Cecil Graham. Hallo, Dumby! I thought you were asleep.

Dumby. I am, I usually am!

Lord Augustus. A very clever woman. Knows perfectly well what a demmed fool I am—knows it as well as I do myself.

[Cecil Graham comes towards him laughing.]

Ah, you may laugh, my boy, but it is a great thing to come across a woman who thoroughly understands one.

Dumby. It is an awfully dangerous thing. They always end by marrying one.

Cecil Graham. But I thought, Tuppy, you were never going to see her again! Yes! you told me so yesterday evening at the club. You said you'd heard—

[Whispering to him.]

Lord Augustus. Oh, she's explained that.

Cecil Graham. And the Wiesbaden affair?

Lord Augustus. She's explained that too.

Dumby. And her income, Tuppy? Has she explained that?

Lord Augustus. [In a very serious voice.] She's going to explain that to-morrow.

[Cecil Graham goes back to C. table.]

Dumby. Awfully commercial, women nowadays. Our grandmothers threw their caps over the mills, of course, but, by Jove, their granddaughters only throw their caps over mills that can raise the wind for them.

Lord Augustus. You want to make her out a wicked woman. She is not!

Cecil Graham. Oh! Wicked women bother one. Good women bore one. That is the only difference between them.

Lord Augustus. [Puffing a cigar.] Mrs. Erlynne has a future before her.

Dumby. Mrs. Erlynne has a past before her.

Lord Augustus. I prefer women with a past. They're always so demmed amusing to talk to.

Cecil Graham. Well, you'll have lots of topics of conversation with her, Tuppy. [Rising and going to him.]

Lord Augustus. You're getting annoying, dear-boy; you're getting demmed annoying.

Cecil Graham. [Puts his hands on his shoulders.] Now, Tuppy, you've lost your figure and you've lost your character. Don't lose your temper; you have only got one.

Lord Augustus. My dear boy, if I wasn't the most good-natured man in London—

Cecil Graham. We'd treat you with more respect, wouldn't we, Tuppy? [Strolls away.]

Dumby. The youth of the present day are quite monstrous. They have absolutely no respect for dyed hair. [Lord Augustus looks round angrily.]

Cecil Graham. Mrs. Erlynne has a very great respect for dear Tuppy.

Dumby. Then Mrs. Erlynne sets an admirable example to the rest of her sex. It is perfectly brutal the way most women nowadays behave to men who are not their husbands.

Lord Windermere. Dumby, you are ridiculous, and Cecil, you let your tongue run away with you. You must leave Mrs. Erlynne alone. You don't really know anything about her, and you're always talking scandal against her.

Cecil Graham. [Coming towards him L.C.] My dear Arthur, I never talk scandal. I only talk gossip.

Lord Windermere. What is the difference between scandal and gossip?

Cecil Graham. Oh! gossip is charming! History is merely gossip. But scandal is gossip made tedious by morality. Now, I never moralise. A man who moralises is usually a hypocrite, and a woman who moralises is invariably plain. There is nothing in the whole world so unbecoming to a woman as a Nonconformist conscience. And most women know it, I'm glad to say.

Lord Augustus. Just my sentiments, dear boy, just my sentiments.

Cecil Graham. Sorry to hear it, Tuppy; whenever people agree with me, I always feel I must be wrong.

Lord Augustus. My dear boy, when I was your age—

Cecil Graham. But you never were, Tuppy, and you never will be. [Goes up C.] I say, Darlington, let us have some cards. You'll play, Arthur, won't you?

Lord Windermere. No, thanks, Cecil.

Dumby. [With a sigh.] Good heavens! how marriage ruins a man! It's as demoralising as cigarettes, and far more expensive.

Cecil Graham. You'll play, of course, Tuppy?

Lord Augustus. [Pouring himself out a brandy and soda at table.] Can't, dear boy. Promised Mrs. Erlynne never to play or drink again.

Cecil Graham. Now, my dear Tuppy, don't be led astray into the paths of virtue. Reformed, you would be perfectly tedious. That is the worst of women. They always want one to be good. And if we are good, when they meet us, they don't love us at all. They like to find us quite irretrievably bad, and to leave us quite unattractively good.

Lord Darlington. [Rising from R. table, where he has been writing letters.] They always do find us bad!

Dumby. I don't think we are bad. I think we are all good, except Tuppy.

Lord Darlington. No, we are all in the gutter, but some of us are looking at the stars. [Sits down at C. table.]

Dumby. We are all in the gutter, but some of us are looking at the stars? Upon my word, you are very romantic to-night, Darlington.

Cecil Graham. Too romantic! You must be in love. Who is the girl?

Lord Darlington. The woman I love is not free, or thinks she isn't. [Glances instinctively at Lord Windermere while he speaks.]

Cecil Graham. A married woman, then! Well, there's nothing in the world like the devotion of a married woman. It's a thing no married man knows anything about.

Lord Darlington. Oh! she doesn't love me. She is a good woman. She is the only good woman I have ever met in my life.

Cecil Graham. The only good woman you have ever met in your life?

Lord Darlington. Yes!

Cecil Graham. [Lighting a cigarette.] Well, you are a lucky fellow! Why, I have met hundreds of good women. I never seem to meet any but good women. The world is perfectly packed with good women. To know them is a middle-class education.

Lord Darlington. This woman has purity and innocence. She has everything we men have lost.

Cecil Graham. My dear fellow, what on earth should we men do going about with purity and innocence? A carefully thought-out buttonhole is much more effective.

Dumby. She doesn't really love you then?

Lord Darlington. No, she does not!

Dumby. I congratulate you, my dear fellow. In this world there are only two tragedies. One is not getting what one wants, and the other is getting it. The last is much the worst; the last is a real tragedy! But I am interested to hear she does not love you. How long could you love a woman who didn't love you, Cecil?

Cecil Graham. A woman who didn't love me? Oh, all my life!

Dumby. So could I. But it's so difficult to meet one.

Lord Darlington. How can you be so conceited, Dumby?

Dumby. I didn't say it as a matter of conceit. I said it as a matter of regret. I have been wildly, madly adored. I am sorry I have. It has been an immense nuisance. I should like to be allowed a little time to myself now and then.

Lord Augustus. [Looking round.] Time to educate yourself, I suppose.

Dumby. No, time to forget all I have learned. That is much more important, dear Tuppy. [Lord Augustus moves uneasily in his chair.]

Lord Darlington. What cynics you fellows are!

Cecil Graham. What is a cynic? [Sitting on the back of the sofa.]

Lord Darlington. A man who knows the price of everything and the value of nothing.

Cecil Graham. And a sentimentalist, my dear Darlington, is a man who sees an absurd value in everything, and doesn't know the market price of any single thing.

Lord Darlington. You always amuse me, Cecil. You talk as if you were a man of experience.

Cecil Graham. I am. [Moves up to front off fireplace.]

Lord Darlington. You are far too young!

Cecil Graham. That is a great error. Experience is a question of instinct about life. I have got it. Tuppy hasn't. Experience is the name Tuppy gives to his mistakes. That is all. [Lord Augustus looks round indignantly.]

Dumby. Experience is the name every one gives to their mistakes.

Cecil Graham. [Standing with his back to the fireplace.] One shouldn't commit any. [Sees Lady Windermere's fan on sofa.]

Dumby. Life would be very dull without them.

Cecil Graham. Of course you are quite faithful to this woman you are in love with, Darlington, to this good woman?

Lord Darlington. Cecil, if one really loves a woman, all other women in the world become absolutely meaningless to one. Love changes one—I am changed.

Cecil Graham. Dear me! How very interesting! Tuppy, I want to talk to you. [Lord Augustus takes no notice.]

Dumby. It's no use talking to Tuppy. You might just as well talk to a brick wall.

Cecil Graham. But I like talking to a brick wall—it's the only thing in the world that never contradicts me! Tuppy!

Lord Augustus. Well, what is it? What is it? [Rising and going over to Cecil Graham.]

Cecil Graham. Come over here. I want you particularly. [Aside.] Darlington has been moralising and talking about the purity of love, and that sort of thing, and he has got some woman in his rooms all the time.

Lord Augustus. No, really! really!

Cecil Graham. [In a low voice.] Yes, here is her fan. [Points to the fan.]

Lord Augustus. [Chuckling.] By Jove! By Jove!

Lord Windermere. [Up by door.] I am really off now, Lord Darlington. I am sorry you are leaving England so soon. Pray call on us when you come back! My wife and I will be charmed to see you!

Lord Darlington. [Upstage with Lord Windermere.] I am afraid I shall be away for many years. Good-night!

Cecil Graham. Arthur!

Lord Windermere. What?

Cecil Graham. I want to speak to you for a moment. No, do come!

Lord Windermere. [Putting on his coat.] I can't—I'm off!

Cecil Graham. It is something very particular. It will interest you enormously.

Lord Windermere. [Smiling.] It is some of your nonsense, Cecil.

Cecil Graham. It isn't! It isn't really.

Lord Augustus. [Going to him.] My dear fellow, you mustn't go yet. I have a lot to talk to you about. And Cecil has something to show you.

Lord Windermere. [Walking over.] Well, what is it?

Cecil Graham. Darlington has got a woman here in his rooms. Here is her fan. Amusing, isn't it? [A pause.]

Lord Windermere. Good God! [Seizes the fan—Dumby rises.]

Cecil Graham. What is the matter?

Lord Windermere. Lord Darlington!

Lord Darlington. [Turning round.] Yes!

Lord Windermere. What is my wife's fan doing here in your rooms? Hands off, Cecil. Don't touch me.

Lord Darlington. Your wife's fan?

Lord Windermere. Yes, here it is!

Lord Darlington. [Walking towards him.] I don't know!

Lord Windermere. You must know. I demand an explanation. Don't hold me, you fool. [To Cecil Graham.]

Lord Darlington. [Aside.] She is here after all!

Lord Windermere. Speak, sir! Why is my wife's fan here? Answer me! By God! I'll search your rooms, and if my wife's here, I'll— [Moves.]

Lord Darlington. You shall not search my rooms. You have no right to do so. I forbid you!

Lord Windermere. You scoundrel! I'll not leave your room till I have searched every corner of it! What moves behind that curtain? [Rushes towards the curtain C.]

Mrs. Erlynne. [Enters behind R.] Lord Windermere!

Lord Windermere. Mrs. Erlynne!

[Every one starts and turns round. Lady Windermere slips out from behind the curtain and glides from the room L.]

Mrs. Erlynne. I am afraid I took your wife's fan in mistake for my own, when I was leaving your house to-night. I am so sorry. [Takes fan from him. Lord Windermere looks at her in contempt. Lord Darlington in mingled astonishment and anger. Lord Augustus turns away. The other men smile at each other.]

Act Drop.

FOURTH ACT

SCENE—Same as in Act I.

Lady Windermere. [Lying on sofa.] How can I tell him? I can't tell him. It would kill me. I wonder what happened after I escaped from that horrible room. Perhaps she told them the true reason of her being there, and the real meaning of that—fatal fan of mine. Oh, if he knows—how can I look him in the face again? He would never forgive me. [Touches bell.] How securely one thinks one lives—out of reach of temptation, sin, folly. And then suddenly—Oh! Life is terrible. It rules us, we do not rule it.

[Enter Rosalie R.]

Rosalie. Did your ladyship ring for me?

Lady Windermere. Yes. Have you found out at what time Lord Windermere came in last night?

Rosalie. His lordship did not come in till five o'clock.

Lady Windermere. Five o'clock? He knocked at my door this morning, didn't he?

Rosalie. Yes, my lady—at half-past nine. I told him your ladyship was not awake yet.

Lady Windermere. Did he say anything?

Rosalie. Something about your ladyship's fan. I didn't quite catch what his lordship said. Has the fan been lost, my lady? I can't find it, and Parker says it was not left in any of the rooms. He has looked in all of them and on the terrace as well.

Lady Windermere. It doesn't matter. Tell Parker not to trouble. That will do.

[Exit Rosalie.]

Lady Windermere. [Rising.] She is sure to tell him. I can fancy a person doing a wonderful act of self-sacrifice, doing it spontaneously, recklessly, nobly—and afterwards finding out that it costs too much. Why should she hesitate between her ruin and mine? . . . How strange! I would have publicly disgraced her in my own house. She accepts public disgrace in the house of another to save me. . . . There is a bitter irony in things, a bitter irony in the way we talk of good and bad women. . . . Oh, what a lesson! and what a pity that in life we only get our lessons when they are of no use to us! For even if she doesn't tell, I must. Oh! the shame of it, the shame of it. To tell it is to live through it all again. Actions are the first tragedy in life, words are the second. Words are perhaps the worst. Words are merciless. . . . Oh! [Starts as Lord Windermere enters.]

Lord Windermere. [Kisses her.] Margaret—how pale you look!

Lady Windermere. I slept very badly.

Lord Windermere. [Sitting on sofa with her.] I am so sorry. I came in dreadfully late, and didn't like to wake you. You are crying, dear.

Lady Windermere. Yes, I am crying, for I have something to tell you, Arthur.

Lord Windermere. My dear child, you are not well. You've been doing too much. Let us go away to the country. You'll be all right at Selby. The season is almost over. There is no use staying on. Poor darling! We'll go away to-day, if you like. [Rises.] We can easily catch the 3.40. I'll send a wire to Fannen. [Crosses and sits down at table to write a telegram.]

Lady Windermere. Yes; let us go away to-day. No; I can't go to-day, Arthur. There is some one I must see before I leave town—some one who has been kind to me.

Lord Windermere. [Rising and leaning over sofa.] Kind to you?

Lady Windermere. Far more than that. [Rises and goes to him.] I will tell you, Arthur, but only love me, love me as you used to love me.

Lord Windermere. Used to? You are not thinking of that wretched woman who came here last night? [Coming round and sitting R. of her.] You don't still imagine—no, you couldn't.

Lady Windermere. I don't. I know now I was wrong and foolish.

Lord Windermere. It was very good of you to receive her last night—but you are never to see her again.

Lady Windermere. Why do you say that? [A pause.]

Lord Windermere. [Holding her hand.] Margaret, I thought Mrs. Erlynne was a woman more sinned against than sinning, as the phrase goes. I thought she wanted to be good, to get back into a place that she had lost by a moment's folly, to lead again a decent life. I believed what she told me—I was mistaken in her. She is bad—as bad as a woman can be.

Lady Windermere. Arthur, Arthur, don't talk so bitterly about any woman. I don't think now that people can be divided into the good and the bad as though they were two separate races or creations. What are called good women may have terrible things in them, mad moods of recklessness, assertion, jealousy, sin. Bad women, as they are termed, may have in them sorrow, repentance, pity, sacrifice. And I don't think Mrs. Erlynne a bad woman—I know she's not.

Lord Windermere. My dear child, the woman's impossible. No matter what harm she tries to do us, you must never see her again. She is inadmissible anywhere.

Lady Windermere. But I want to see her. I want her to come here.

Lord Windermere. Never!

Lady Windermere. She came here once as your guest. She must come now as mine. That is but fair.

Lord Windermere. She should never have come here.

Lady Windermere. [Rising.] It is too late, Arthur, to say that now. [Moves away.]

Lord Windermere. [Rising.] Margaret, if you knew where Mrs. Erlynne went last night, after she left this house, you would not sit in the same room with her. It was absolutely shameless, the whole thing.

Lady Windermere. Arthur, I can't bear it any longer. I must tell you. Last night—

[Enter Parker with a tray on which lie Lady Windermere's fan and a card.]

Parker. Mrs. Erlynne has called to return your ladyship's fan which she took away by mistake last night. Mrs. Erlynne has written a message on the card.

Lady Windermere. Oh, ask Mrs. Erlynne to be kind enough to come up. [Reads card.] Say I shall be very glad to see her.

[Exit Parker.]

She wants to see me, Arthur.

Lord Windermere. [Takes card and looks at it.] Margaret, I beg you not to. Let me see her first, at any rate. She's a very dangerous woman. She is the most dangerous woman I know. You don't realise what you're doing.

Lady Windermere. It is right that I should see her.

Lord Windermere. My child, you may be on the brink of a great sorrow. Don't go to meet it. It is absolutely necessary that I should see her before you do.

Lady Windermere. Why should it be necessary?

[Enter Parker.]

Parker. Mrs. Erlynne.

[Enter Mrs. Erlynne.]

[Exit Parker.]

Mrs. Erlynne. How do you do, Lady Windermere? [To Lord Windermere.] How do you do? Do you know, Lady Windermere, I am so sorry about your fan. I can't imagine how I made such a silly mistake. Most stupid of me. And as I was driving in your direction, I thought I would take the opportunity of returning your property in person with many apologies for my carelessness, and of bidding you good-bye.

Lady Windermere. Good-bye? [Moves towards sofa with Mrs. Erlynne and sits down beside her.] Are you going away, then, Mrs. Erlynne?

Mrs. Erlynne. Yes; I am going to live abroad again. The English climate doesn't suit me. My—heart is affected here, and that I don't like. I prefer living in the south. London is too full of fogs and—and serious people, Lord Windermere. Whether the fogs produce the serious people or whether the serious people produce the fogs, I don't know, but the whole thing rather gets on my nerves, and so I'm leaving this afternoon by the Club Train.

Lady Windermere. This afternoon? But I wanted so much to come and see you.

Mrs. Erlynne. How kind of you! But I am afraid I have to go.

Lady Windermere. Shall I never see you again, Mrs. Erlynne?

Mrs. Erlynne. I am afraid not. Our lives lie too far apart. But there is a little thing I would like you to do for me. I want a photograph of you, Lady Windermere—would you give me one? You don't know how gratified I should be.

Lady Windermere. Oh, with pleasure. There is one on that table. I'll show it to you. [Goes across to the table.]

Lord Windermere. [Coming up to Mrs. Erlynne and speaking in a low voice.] It is monstrous your intruding yourself here after your conduct last night.

Mrs. Erlynne. [With an amused smile.] My dear Windermere, manners before morals!

Lady Windermere. [Returning.] I'm afraid it is very flattering—I am not so pretty as that. [Showing photograph.]

Mrs. Erlynne. You are much prettier. But haven't you got one of yourself with your little boy?

Lady Windermere. I have. Would you prefer one of those?

Mrs. Erlynne. Yes.

Lady Windermere. I'll go and get it for you, if you'll excuse me for a moment. I have one upstairs.

Mrs. Erlynne. So sorry, Lady Windermere, to give you so much trouble.

Lady Windermere. [Moves to door R.] No trouble at all, Mrs. Erlynne.

Mrs. Erlynne. Thanks so much.

[Exit Lady Windermere R.] You seem rather out of temper this morning, Windermere. Why should you be? Margaret and I get on charmingly together.

Lord Windermere. I can't bear to see you with her. Besides, you have not told me the truth, Mrs. Erlynne.

Mrs. Erlynne. I have not told her the truth, you mean.

Lord Windermere. [Standing C.] I sometimes wish you had. I should have been spared then the misery, the anxiety, the annoyance of the last six months. But rather than my wife should know—that the mother whom she was taught to consider as dead, the mother whom she has mourned as dead, is living—a divorced woman, going about under an assumed name, a bad woman preying upon life, as I know you now to be—rather than that, I was ready to supply you with money to pay bill after bill, extravagance after extravagance, to risk what occurred yesterday, the first quarrel I have ever had with my wife. You don't understand what that means to me. How could you? But I tell you that the only bitter words that ever came from those sweet lips of hers were on your account, and I hate to see you next her. You sully the innocence that is in her. [Moves L.C.] And then I used to think that with all your faults you were frank and honest. You are not.

Mrs. Erlynne. Why do you say that?

Lord Windermere. You made me get you an invitation to my wife's ball.

Mrs. Erlynne. For my daughter's ball—yes.

Lord Windermere. You came, and within an hour of your leaving the house you are found in a man's rooms—you are disgraced before every one. [Goes up stage C.]

Mrs. Erlynne. Yes.

Lord Windermere. [Turning round on her.] Therefore I have a right to look upon you as what you are—a worthless, vicious woman. I have the right to tell you never to enter this house, never to attempt to come near my wife—

Mrs. Erlynne. [Coldly.] My daughter, you mean.

Lord Windermere. You have no right to claim her as your daughter. You left her, abandoned her when she was but a child in the cradle, abandoned her for your lover, who abandoned you in turn.

Mrs. Erlynne. [Rising.] Do you count that to his credit, Lord Windermere—or to mine?

Lord Windermere. To his, now that I know you.

Mrs. Erlynne. Take care—you had better be careful.

Lord Windermere. Oh, I am not going to mince words for you. I know you thoroughly.

Mrs. Erlynne. [Looks steadily at him.] I question that.

Lord Windermere. I do know you. For twenty years of your life you lived without your child, without a thought of your child. One day you read in the papers that she had married a rich man. You saw your hideous chance. You knew that to spare her the ignominy of learning that a woman like you was her mother, I would endure anything. You began your blackmailing.

Mrs. Erlynne. [Shrugging her shoulders.] Don't use ugly words, Windermere. They are vulgar. I saw my chance, it is true, and took it.

Lord Windermere. Yes, you took it—and spoiled it all last night by being found out.

Mrs. Erlynne. [With a strange smile.] You are quite right, I spoiled it all last night.

Lord Windermere. And as for your blunder in taking my wife's fan from here and then leaving it about in Darlington's rooms, it is unpardonable. I can't bear the sight of it now. I shall never let my wife use it again. The thing is soiled for me. You should have kept it and not brought it back.

Mrs. Erlynne. I think I shall keep it. [Goes up.] It's extremely pretty. [Takes up fan.] I shall ask Margaret to give it to me.

Lord Windermere. I hope my wife will give it you.

Mrs. Erlynne. Oh, I'm sure she will have no objection.

Lord Windermere. I wish that at the same time she would give you a miniature she kisses every night before she prays—It's the miniature of a young innocent-looking girl with beautiful dark hair.

Mrs. Erlynne. Ah, yes, I remember. How long ago that seems! [Goes to sofa and sits down.] It was done before I was married. Dark hair and an innocent expression were the fashion then, Windermere! [A pause.]

Lord Windermere. What do you mean by coming here this morning? What is your object? [Crossing L.C. and sitting.]

Mrs. Erlynne. [With a note of irony in her voice.] To bid good-bye to my dear daughter, of course. [Lord Windermere bites his under lip in anger. Mrs. Erlynne looks at him, and her voice and manner become serious. In her accents as she talks there is a note of deep tragedy. For a moment she reveals herself.] Oh, don't imagine I am going to have a pathetic scene with her, weep on her neck and tell her who I am, and all that kind of thing. I have no ambition to play the part of a mother. Only once in my life have I known a mother's feelings. That was last night. They were terrible—they made me suffer—they made me suffer too much. For twenty years, as you say, I have lived childless,—I want to live childless still. [Hiding her feelings with a trivial laugh.] Besides, my dear Windermere, how on earth could I pose as a mother with a grown-up daughter? Margaret is twenty-one, and I have never admitted that I am more than twenty-nine, or thirty at the most. Twenty-nine when there are pink shades, thirty when there are not. So you see what difficulties it would involve. No, as far as I am concerned, let your wife cherish the memory of this dead, stainless mother. Why should I interfere with her illusions? I find it hard enough to keep my own. I lost one illusion last night. I thought I had no heart. I find I have, and a heart doesn't suit me, Windermere. Somehow it doesn't go with modern dress. It makes one look old. [Takes up hand-mirror from table and looks into it.] And it spoils one's career at critical moments.

Lord Windermere. You fill me with horror—with absolute horror.

Mrs. Erlynne. [Rising.] I suppose, Windermere, you would like me to retire into a convent, or become a hospital nurse, or something of that kind, as people do in silly modern novels. That is stupid of you, Arthur; in real life we don't do such things—not as long as we have any good looks left, at any rate. No—what consoles one nowadays is not repentance, but pleasure. Repentance is quite out of date. And besides, if a woman really repents, she has to go to a bad dressmaker, otherwise no one believes in her. And nothing in the world would induce me to do that. No; I am going to pass entirely out of your two lives. My coming into them has been a mistake—I discovered that last night.

Lord Windermere. A fatal mistake.

Mrs. Erlynne. [Smiling.] Almost fatal.

Lord Windermere. I am sorry now I did not tell my wife the whole thing at once.

Mrs. Erlynne. I regret my bad actions. You regret your good ones—that is the difference between us.

Lord Windermere. I don't trust you. I will tell my wife. It's better for her to know, and from me. It will cause her infinite pain—it will humiliate her terribly, but it's right that she should know.

Mrs. Erlynne. You propose to tell her?

Lord Windermere. I am going to tell her.

Mrs. Erlynne. [Going up to him.] If you do, I will make my name so infamous that it will mar every moment of her life. It will ruin her, and make her wretched. If you dare to tell her, there is no depth of degradation I will not sink to, no pit of shame I will not enter. You shall not tell her—I forbid you.

Lord Windermere. Why?

Mrs. Erlynne. [After a pause.] If I said to you that I cared for her, perhaps loved her even—you would sneer at me, wouldn't you?

Lord Windermere. I should feel it was not true. A mother's love means devotion, unselfishness, sacrifice. What could you know of such things?

Mrs. Erlynne. You are right. What could I know of such things? Don't let us talk any more about it—as for telling my daughter who I am, that I do not allow. It is my secret, it is not yours. If I make up my mind to tell her, and I think I will, I shall tell her before I leave the house—if not, I shall never tell her.

Lord Windermere. [Angrily.] Then let me beg of you to leave our house at once. I will make your excuses to Margaret.

[Enter Lady Windermere R. She goes over to Mrs. Erlynne with the photograph in her hand. Lord Windermere moves to back of sofa, and anxiously watches Mrs. Erlynne as the scene progresses.]

Lady Windermere. I am so sorry, Mrs. Erlynne, to have kept you waiting. I couldn't find the photograph anywhere. At last I discovered it in my husband's dressing-room—he had stolen it.

Mrs. Erlynne. [Takes the photograph from her and looks at it.] I am not surprised—it is charming. [Goes over to sofa with Lady Windermere, and sits down beside her. Looks again at the photograph.] And so that is your little boy! What is he called?

Lady Windermere. Gerard, after my dear father.

Mrs. Erlynne. [Laying the photograph down.] Really?

Lady Windermere. Yes. If it had been a girl, I would have called it after my mother. My mother had the same name as myself, Margaret.

Mrs. Erlynne. My name is Margaret too.

Lady Windermere. Indeed!

Mrs. Erlynne. Yes. [Pause.] You are devoted to your mother's memory, Lady Windermere, your husband tells me.

Lady Windermere. We all have ideals in life. At least we all should have. Mine is my mother.

Mrs. Erlynne. Ideals are dangerous things. Realities are better. They wound, but they're better.

Lady Windermere. [Shaking her head.] If I lost my ideals, I should lose everything.

Mrs. Erlynne. Everything?

Lady Windermere. Yes. [Pause.]

Mrs. Erlynne. Did your father often speak to you of your mother?

Lady Windermere. No, it gave him too much pain. He told me how my mother had died a few months after I was born. His eyes filled with tears as he spoke. Then he begged me never to mention her name to him again. It made him suffer even to hear it. My father—my father really died of a broken heart. His was the most ruined life know.

Mrs. Erlynne. [Rising.] I am afraid I must go now, Lady Windermere.

Lady Windermere. [Rising.] Oh no, don't.

Mrs. Erlynne. I think I had better. My carriage must have come back by this time. I sent it to Lady Jedburgh's with a note.

Lady Windermere. Arthur, would you mind seeing if Mrs. Erlynne's carriage has come back?

Mrs. Erlynne. Pray don't trouble, Lord Windermere.

Lady Windermere. Yes, Arthur, do go, please.

[Lord Windermere hesitated for a moment and looks at Mrs. Erlynne. She remains quite impassive. He leaves the room.]

[To Mrs. Erlynne.] Oh! What am I to say to you? You saved me last night? [Goes towards her.]

Mrs. Erlynne. Hush—don't speak of it.

Lady Windermere. I must speak of it. I can't let you think that I am going to accept this sacrifice. I am not. It is too great. I am going to tell my husband everything. It is my duty.

Mrs. Erlynne. It is not your duty—at least you have duties to others besides him. You say you owe me something?

Lady Windermere. I owe you everything.

Mrs. Erlynne. Then pay your debt by silence. That is the only way in which it can be paid. Don't spoil the one good thing I have done in my life by telling it to any one. Promise me that what passed last night will remain a secret between us. You must not bring misery into your husband's life. Why spoil his love? You must not spoil it. Love is easily killed. Oh! how easily love is killed. Pledge me your word, Lady Windermere, that you will never tell him. I insist upon it.

Lady Windermere. [With bowed head.] It is your will, not mine.

Mrs. Erlynne. Yes, it is my will. And never forget your child—I like to think of you as a mother. I like you to think of yourself as one.

Lady Windermere. [Looking up.] I always will now. Only once in my life I have forgotten my own mother—that was last night. Oh, if I had remembered her I should not have been so foolish, so wicked.

Mrs. Erlynne. [With a slight shudder.] Hush, last night is quite over.

[Enter Lord Windermere.]

Lord Windermere. Your carriage has not come back yet, Mrs. Erlynne.

Mrs. Erlynne. It makes no matter. I'll take a hansom. There is nothing in the world so respectable as a good Shrewsbury and Talbot. And now, dear Lady Windermere, I am afraid it is really good-bye. [Moves up C.] Oh, I remember. You'll think me absurd, but do you know I've taken a great fancy to this fan that I was silly enough to run away with last night from your ball. Now, I wonder would you give it to me? Lord Windermere says you may. I know it is his present.

Lady Windermere. Oh, certainly, if it will give you any pleasure. But it has my name on it. It has 'Margaret' on it.

Mrs. Erlynne. But we have the same Christian name.

Lady Windermere. Oh, I forgot. Of course, do have it. What a wonderful chance our names being the same!

Mrs. Erlynne. Quite wonderful. Thanks—it will always remind me of you. [Shakes hands with her.]

[Enter Parker.]

Parker. Lord Augustus Lorton. Mrs. Erlynne's carriage has come.

[Enter Lord Augustus.]

Lord Augustus. Good morning, dear boy. Good morning, Lady Windermere. [Sees Mrs. Erlynne.] Mrs. Erlynne!

Mrs. Erlynne. How do you do, Lord Augustus? Are you quite well this morning?

Lord Augustus. [Coldly.] Quite well, thank you, Mrs. Erlynne.

Mrs. Erlynne. You don't look at all well, Lord Augustus. You stop up too late—it is so bad for you. You really should take more care of yourself. Good-bye, Lord Windermere. [Goes towards door with a bow to Lord Augustus. Suddenly smiles and looks back at him.] Lord Augustus! Won't you see me to my carriage? You might carry the fan.

Lord Windermere. Allow me!

Mrs. Erlynne. No; I want Lord Augustus. I have a special message for the dear Duchess. Won't you carry the fan, Lord Augustus?

Lord Augustus. If you really desire it, Mrs. Erlynne.

Mrs. Erlynne. [Laughing.] Of course I do. You'll carry it so gracefully. You would carry off anything gracefully, dear Lord Augustus.

[When she reaches the door she looks back for a moment at Lady Windermere. Their eyes meet. Then she turns, and exit C. followed by Lord Augustus.]

Lady Windermere. You will never speak against Mrs. Erlynne again, Arthur, will you?

Lord Windermere. [Gravely.] She is better than one thought her.

Lady Windermere. She is better than I am.

Lord Windermere. [Smiling as he strokes her hair.] Child, you and she belong to different worlds. Into your world evil has never entered.

Lady Windermere. Don't say that, Arthur. There is the same world for all of us, and good and evil, sin and innocence, go through it hand in hand. To shut one's eyes to half of life that one may live securely is as though one blinded oneself that one might walk with more safety in a land of pit and precipice.

Lord Windermere. [Moves down with her.] Darling, why do you say that?

Lady Windermere. [Sits on sofa.] Because I, who had shut my eyes to life, came to the brink. And one who had separated us—

Lord Windermere. We were never separated.

Lady Windermere. We never must be again. O Arthur, don't love me less, and I will trust you more. I will trust you absolutely. Let us go to Selby. In the Rose Garden at Selby the roses are white and red.

[Enter Lord Augustus C.]

Lord Augustus. Arthur, she has explained everything!

[Lady Windermere looks horribly frightened at this. Lord Windermere starts. Lord Augustus takes Windermere by the arm and brings him to front of stage. He talks rapidly and in a low voice. Lady Windermere stands watching them in terror.] My dear fellow, she has explained every demmed thing. We all wronged her immensely. It was entirely for my sake she went to Darlington's rooms. Called first at the Club—fact is, wanted to put me out of suspense—and being told I had gone on—followed—naturally frightened when she heard a lot of us coming in—retired to another room—I assure you, most gratifying to me, the whole thing. We all behaved brutally to her. She is just the woman for me. Suits me down to the ground. All the conditions she makes are that we live entirely out of England. A very good thing too. Demmed clubs, demmed climate, demmed cooks, demmed everything. Sick of it all!

Lady Windermere. [Frightened.] Has Mrs. Erlynne—?

Lord Augustus. [Advancing towards her with a low bow.] Yes, Lady Windermere— Mrs. Erlynne has done me the honour of accepting my hand.

Lord Windermere. Well, you are certainly marrying a very clever woman!

Lady Windermere. [Taking her husband's hand.] Ah, you're marrying a very good woman!

Curtain